CHARACTER PIECES
in Romantic Style

12 Short Piano Solos

MARTHA MIER

Character pieces are short piano works that most often communicate a single emotion or idea, such as the joy of spring or the image of a child falling asleep. Composers first began writing character pieces in the 19th century, during the Romantic period, as a personal, inward-looking form of musical expression, on a smaller scale than the lengthy and highly structured sonatas of the Classical period. Many of the Romantic-period composers created character pieces. Important collections include the *Scenes from Childhood*, Op. 15, by Robert Schumann and the *Songs Without Words* by Felix Mendelssohn. My goal in writing *Character Pieces in Romantic Style* was to create new character pieces carefully graded for students that emulate this important art form from the Romantic period. Some of the pieces are bold in character, while others are lyrical and introspective. These moods are suggested by each title. I hope students enjoy exploring these pieces and use them to develop musical, imaginative playing.

Martha Mier

Alfred Music
P.O. Box 10003
Van Nuys, CA 91410-0003
alfred.com

ISBN-10: 1-4706-4144-5
ISBN-13: 978-1-4706-4144-3

Cover art: Beautiful Pantone-coloured hues © Getty Images / LeslieLauren

Beneath the Stars

Martha Mier

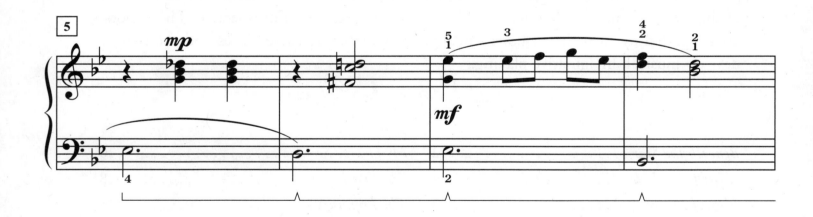

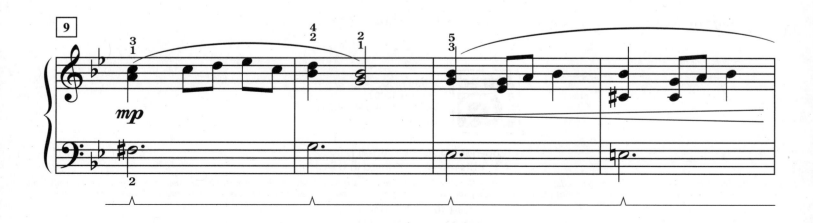

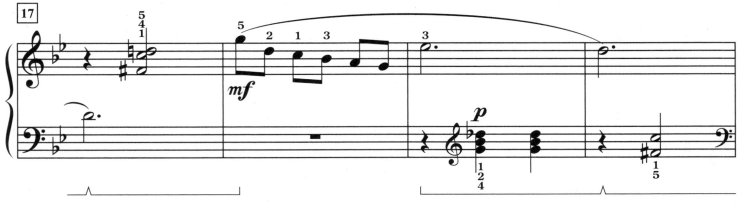

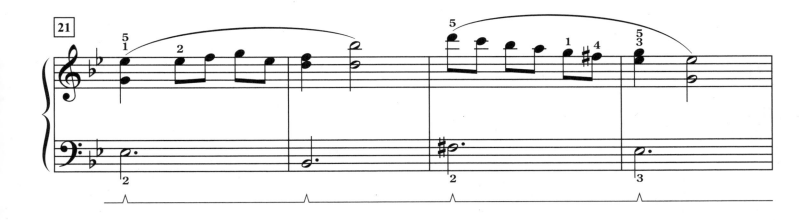

TRANQUILITY

Martha Mier

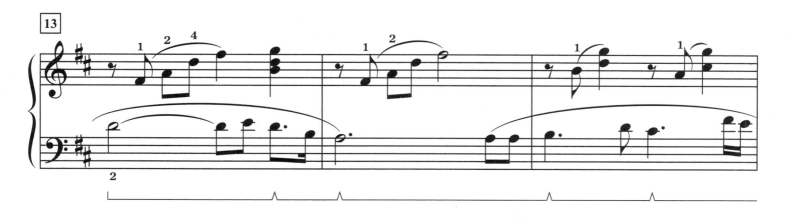

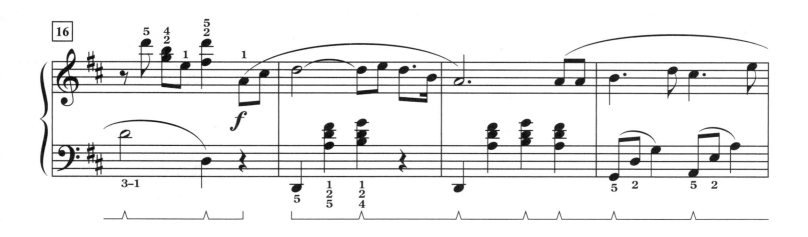

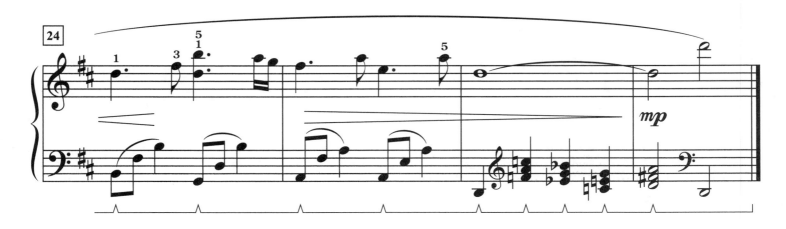

REVERIE

Martha Mier

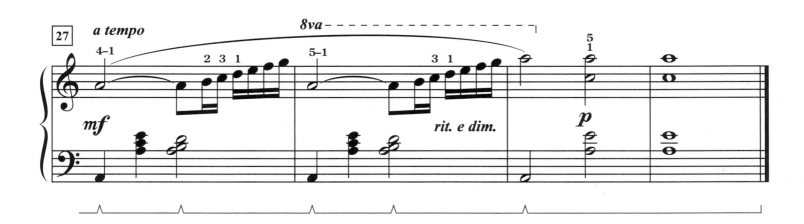

THE OLD DIARY

Martha Mier

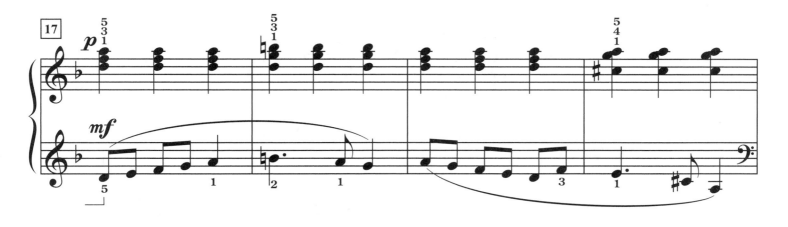

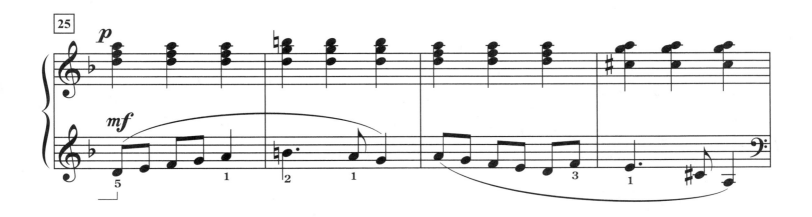

MY HEART'S SECRET

Martha Mier

SUMMER LOVE

Martha Mier

HUMMINGBIRDS AT PLAY

Martha Mier

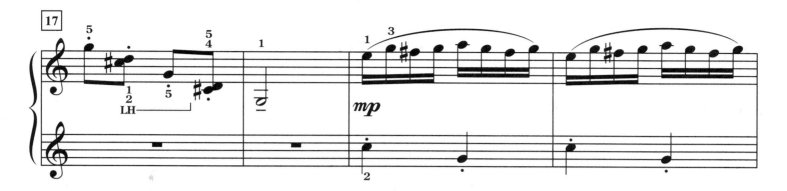

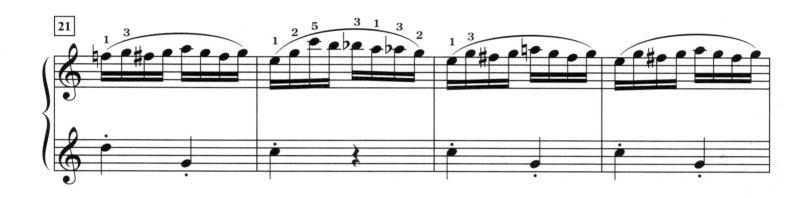

Majestic Iceberg

Martha Mier

THE PROMISE

Martha Mier

ELEGANT DANCE

Martha Mier

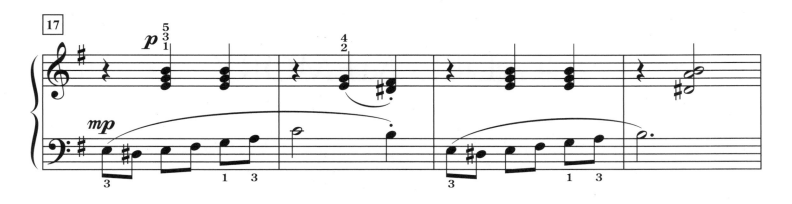

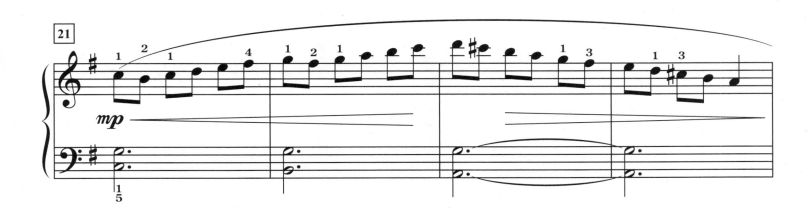

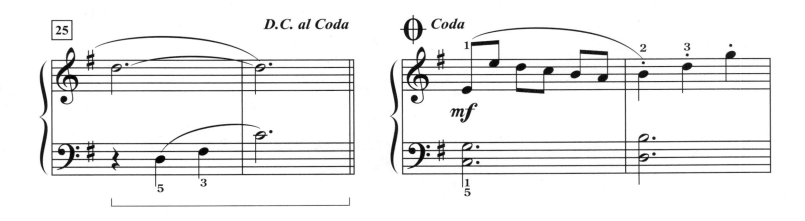

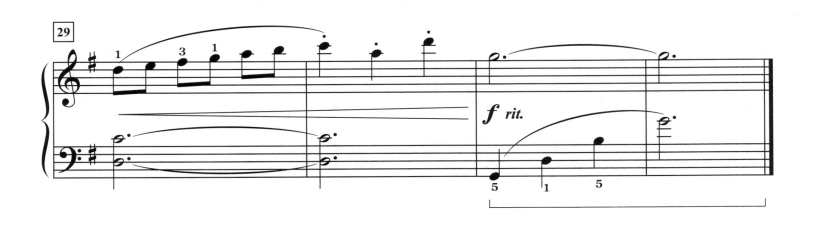

A FADED MEMORY

Martha Mier

A Brief Interlude

Martha Mier